Divine
Nothingness

In Beauty Bright

Stealing History

Early Collected Poems: 1965–1992

What I Can't Bear Losing: Notes from a Life

Save the Last Dance

Everything Is Burning

Not God After All

American Sonnets

Last Blue

This Time: New and Selected Poems

Odd Mercy

Bread Without Sugar

Two Long Poems

Leaving Another Kingdom

Lovesick

Paradise Poems

The Red Coal

Lucky Life

Rejoicings

The Naming of Beasts

The Pineys

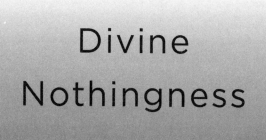

Divine Nothingness

POEMS

Gerald Stern

W. W. NORTON & COMPANY

NEW YORK   LONDON

For information about permission to reproduce selections from this
book, write to Permissions, W. W. Norton & Company, Inc.,
500 Fifth Avenue, New York, NY 10110

For information about special discounts for bulk purchases, please
contact W. W. Norton Special Sales at specialsales@wwnorton.com
or 800-233-4830

Manufacturing by Courier Westford
Production manager: Louise Parasmo

Library of Congress Cataloging-in-Publication Data

Stern, Gerald, date.
[Poems Selections]
Divine nothingness : poems / Gerald Stern.
  ISBN 978-0-393-24350-5 (hardcover)
1. Life—Poetry. 2. Mortality—Poetry. I. Title.
PS3569.T3888A6 2015
811'.54—dc23
                                        2014017818

W. W. Norton & Company, Inc.
500 Fifth Avenue, New York, NY 10110
www.wwnorton.com

W. W. Norton & Company Ltd.
Castle House, 75/76 Wells Street, London W1T3QT

1 2 3 4 5 6 7 8 9 0

For Phil and Franny Levine
and for
Charlie Williams and Catherine Mauger

Contents

PART II

PART III

Acknowledgments

I want to acknowledge the terrific work that my assistant, Stephanie Smith, has done in terms of the production of this book and all the prior work that went into the making of it.

Grateful acknowledgment is made to the editors of the following publications, where these poems originally appeared:

The American Poetry Review: "Bio IV," "Bio V," "Swamp Maple," "Ruth," "Possum," "Dolly," "D.," "Wilderness," "Tract," "Not Me," "Cardboard," "What Happened to G.S."

Boulevard: "Daisy," "Home," "At Last"

Colorado Review: "Mule"

FIELD: "Santiago," "Walt's," "Oaxaca," "After the Church Reading Against the War"

The Georgia Review: "Wind and Water," "Sexual"

The Great River Review: "Red Wool Bathrobe," "Manure Spreader," "Havanese," "Durante," "I'll Be Around"

Miramar: "Love," "Hell," "After Ritsos"

The New Yorker: "Medicinal," "The World We Should Have Stayed In," "What Brings Me Here?"

Poetry: "Much Better Than a Goat"

West 10th: "Little King," "Limping"

Part I

Bio IV

I created an unassailable Utopia amidst Max Factor the powder
and sang such that I entertained a small living room
full mostly of berouged women in the days of Bobbie Breen,
and played for money nine-ball instead of reading Kant
offering my substance to suffer by inattention and suffer
again by the final wiping out of the cosmic mirror.

And I fought Figgy Dutch the toughest when I was only ten
and then again when I was twenty but never once
though I had a gift did I pluck his red eye out,
which brought me to my kitchen window in the autumn of many a year
and many a cat hiding behind the orange and purple chrysanthemums
and one time blue not far from the birdbath his blue Santiago.

I stood there thinking not of Kant but of Paul Goodman though more
    of Delmore Schwartz and even more of John Berryman have you
    heard the terrible news?
Though ten years earlier I sat on a heated glass floor in stack after stack
for the government loved me and gave me more time than you can
    imagine,
which I used wisely not ever sleeping not ever joining the
Communist Party eating supper for a maximum of sixty cents a plate.

Crossroads I had but it meant nothing and though I went
left and right I only followed a thumbtack, and it's
amazing how I didn't die, three times, and where I woke up
and what the dogs said and how I thought Immanuel Kant
would clear the air for me for I heard it somewhere
and followed that thumbtack wherever I thought it would

take me by holding his book under my armpit
through the tunnels and up the evil hills,
beloved hills, and read in bars and restaurants,
and once in the North Side bibliotheque oh Scotchman oh beard
of ages nor was I ever deprived—I couldn't be deprived—
and if I dropped my Air Corps khakis down the incinerator

I never dropped my thumbtack into whose steel or tin
but shining I primped or at least I stared while waiting
for a light or waiting for a drink or looking through
my set of keys (I have eight) in the act of opening
one of my doors (I have three) which is
one of my numbers as eight is the other since I am

occult, though you'd never know it, and willing
to imitate the believer the lover, which isn't
mockery but putting on the dead clothes and giving them life by
climbing or just by breathing as we breathe into a paper bag
or into what we call rubber since our lungs are pumps
and we do the motion of arms and legs as with a threadbare

tire the left hand fitting it into place the right hand
holding the bumper jack a shoulder even
keeping the car upright the smell of birds
escaping from the woods my good luck to find
two bricks to keep the car from rolling, birdfoot
violets for luxury a gust of wind for love.

Bio V

Keep in mind how callow I was and how
sarcastic walking down that dirt road
with no room in any of my outside pockets
for your leftover straw or the gold leaf you gave me
for high achievement in the art of ridicule.

I am what I am is neither substantial nor insubstantial,
non é vero? And who knows how Popeye's creator
found the words and where he heard them, for he was
a Hittite, his name was Segar, or Siegel, a bird by the
way of Hittite persuasion whose name at the seashore
and many an inland river is Seagull, a dull
joke among the Floridians who gathered
to fish from the wooden pier and play shuffleboard
in the sun among the discs their blue Santiago.

And keep in mind how hard it was to stand
in the rain and listen to music holding a tin
basin over your head, for who had money then
to buy an umbrella or even a *Sun-Telegraph*,
and who had money to buy a steak, the piece
of meat we glorified, a cow's fat ass,
or his rib or his shoulder, cooked in salty butter?

Rant till you die, but keep in mind one Sunday
you went with someone named Susan to an African-
Methodist church in Iowa City and sang
for over an hour and listened to a reading
from Deuteronomy a famous section and
heard the sermon and walked out wet-eyed for you were
foolish then and Susan was even worse.

And where your rabbi is buried
and how you talked for hours about which cemetery
you'd go to but she died first though decades younger
and though her hill has a pine tree and even catches
the wind, it's your voices that count the most,
that salad of chopped-up lettuce engulfed in tuna
the two of you spent three hours over, the subject
death, and what the Hittite nose was like,
and how Jeremiah will sound when he comes back
and what would he do in Camden or East St. Louis
and could they hear him break another glass bottle
and could they bear his curses perish the day,
the noisy geese in formation too late maybe,
my own steps icy, Thelonious Monk playing
Duke Ellington in the small living room
and underneath that the "Unaccompanied Cello,"
consideration in the green kitchen and almost
kindness on the dedicated shelf,
entwined pigs and a rooster, if you can stand it.

SWAMP MAPLE

All I could think of was playing Chopin for you
while you took off your bra by reaching under
and slept through one prelude after another
both that night and the next, and it was my blood
you wiped with a towel and it was a piece of birch
I brought with me to make the matter worse,
and drew bisons for you and when you let me
I buried my face in yours for I was immersed
and wrote on the soft inside and even rubbed
my chin with it—you've seen a horse rolling
over and over, did you ever watch a cat tearing
the wet grass, did you ever see a blue jay
wait for the roar before she dove into the swamp maple?

SANTIAGO

So much for owning your own limousine
and running around to open the door
and wearing a short oh green and blossoming necktie
they always wore in the panic they called a Panic
where things were things nor was it even a *thing*—
that limousine—though my car was a green
fifteen-year-old Buick, a strip on the windshield
and two broken springs in the back for passengers
and no necktie anywhere not to mention
a hat with a bill or a hat with a turkey feather
or a screaming turkey under my arm, a thing
if I ever saw one, brown and obtrusive, with
a blood-filled wattle and legs that scratched
and wings that had an amazing body—just
a thought passing the 1939 World's Fair on
my way to Kennedy my first stop for Santiago.

RUTH

There was a way I could find out if Ruth
were still alive but it said nothing about
her '46 Mercury nor how the gear shift ruined
our making love nor how her brother found her
compromised and what the contempt was
he registered, though I wanted to remember
the two hundred steps I climbed and the first
kisses in the empty kitchen a lifetime
before she died of emphysema and all
her credits were spread out on a page
in what they called an "almanac" for which
I chose to walk uphill for a half hour
until I reached a house with a blue boat
in the front yard, then walk back down for downhill
you are relieved since you have a whole city
below you and you have the wind at your back
for consolation and a small porcupine
at home in the empty street and hunched over
eating a rotten cabbage since grief is your subject.

POSSUM

I'd rather believe it was only chance that put the opossum
into my garbage can and he lay dead inside
from too many peelings and drowned from too many smells,
and he was like a cat in size which shocked me
and he came back from the dead, if I can say that
and crawled out as soon as it got dark
and a weird sense told him Rebecca wasn't looking
and we named him Lazarus to show that we loved him
and when he wanted to play we all lay down dead
just to show that humans are good at that too
or maybe he wasn't playing and he had the same
longings we did or maybe he was studying
how *we* died, some of us just slumped over,
some of us lying with grave and cradled heads,
and some of us turned into stone like standing ghosts,
though he may have had rabies and we were just lucky.

WALT'S

I stopped for peaches at the bridge but no one
was there since it was ten at night and it was
dark underneath the trees and there were two
wagonloads and a cash box and a scale
but no one had indicated the price though there were
plastic bags and my hands were shaking when I
put the money in the box. I made it
a dollar a pound but that was too low for peaches
like that and I had already stopped
on the bridge with my motor running to look down
at the river and it was too late to go back and how
could I explain it, say, to a twenty-year-old
with a strap underneath his chin and the sickening lights
going on and off and how in the world does it
compare anyway to Moses taking the law
into his own hands and murdering the Egyptian?

DAISY

Who says who's the master and whom and whither
and if love is an airborne thing
and we leave doors and windows open
and the rooms are adrift with pollen-druff
and beetle-husk and skullock-motes,
and where Daisy is, that donkey
and who does she belong to
and would she be good enough to ride
in my homecoming down Wylie Avenue
and should flowers be on her head or mine
and if it's decent enough to bring her into the Gaslight
or for that matter into the Crawford Grill.

DOLLY

It's true that in spite of the sign that said
no dogs or else
I was offered a room under the weather vane
where the arrow's shadow came and went and
there was a mattress against the wall
and boxes of records and cartons of lightbulbs
and Dolly whom I hid in a shopping bag
only allowed herself to whimper
for dogs know when it's time to hide
and, for all I know, can read our miserable signs
and what you do with a dog in a shopping bag
you can gently hold her mouth shut
for she wants to bark
and that would ruin your nap on the filthy mattress
and later your swim
and most of all near the ivy and the beach plum
the race to restore knowledge with a stick.

LITTLE KING

At last an electric fence so I can be safe from the deer for a minute
and dig a deep hole under the props so I can sneak in like a weasel
but nobody loves me enough to bring me a scotch on ice as in the
   old days
and we may as well be in Norway how it's 2 a.m. and I'm sitting
in an Adirondack chair by a pool of water under a cherry tree
for it's never night but forty times worse than that it's never day;
and at a certain point in more than one country
there is a day given over to pure confusion, which
if you had any sense you would skip, weasel or no weasel,
electric fence or no, Mongolian, Neanderthal, orangutan,
black and white sheep hound or no, even if the pool is heated
even if the cherries are sweet, even if a wolf
with too much milk started the agonies in the first place,
even if the Little King drives by in a twelve-cylinder 1920 Packard
and has a stepladder.

D.

My Deborah was a judge too
only I am pulling names out of a hat
the way you did rabbits

and though she stood with her toes pointed in
as if she were in the docks
she was still the judge and would remain one.

There is only one other person who understands this,
the rest will have to go by language alone.

Think of a meadowlark you held in the cup of your hands
and how you reached down to kiss her wet feathers
and she bit you twice, on the lip and the left cheek.

From Rome

From Rome comes Apollinaire
and from America comes the little hummingbird
but don't worry your beaten-down heart,
he will live on the three *Quais*
along with the leftover Romanians
and Simone de Beauvoir Chicago wife,
she who brought the leather pouch of tiny eggs,
and smeared her lips with bee balm on her own bridge
and longed for American drug stores
so she could eat breakfast in the *parfumes* there.

HOME

As my cousin Norman used to say
Jerry always had the brains in the family
though I think it was the interest rate was high
and Stern's Realty was just a desk at twilight,
so let me take you back to the meadow
where the sidewalk suddenly became a river
as one street rounded a bend and then another,
and thank your Hebrew stars
there wasn't an Automat there to drool over
or a soft-shell crab dinner that cost
only two seventy-five a plate
just before everything went high-sky
and everyone had a sideline, trapping crows
to get at their blood, wearing
a tape measure over their shoulders for a shawl.

At Last

Time was getting shorter every year
and we broke into sound the slightest touch of the
feather duster and we had bricks up our sleeves
you can't imagine and climbed three steps at a time—
though one of the versions was we never got there
or one of us got there first by banging the dashboard.

But *I'd* say it was getting there and not getting there
and banging had nothing to do with it
except it was Etta James if that means anything
and it was a kind of reunion after twenty
minutes of silence and we
sang together though they were different songs.

Red Wool Bathrobe

When the sirens didn't let up outside his
window for even a minute he closed his eyes
and started to count for that was the night he just
couldn't sleep and when that happens he puts on
his red wool bathrobe torn in both sleeves
and being where he is in this life he only
has pleasure lying there remembering the
second floor of the old Pillsbury building
where the former cleaner hung the unclaimed
clothing in rows from God knows when including
the bathrobe with a rusty safety pin
still holding the ticket and it would have done so for eight
more years until the church next door expanded
and that was one thing quickly becoming another
yet keeping space for the dark and uncanny
for God loves his sleepless creatures.

FORT PITT HOTEL

We like to talk about the word—
it makes us feel we were there in the beginning—
but it was neither in New York City
nor on the boat going back and forth all night
nor was it the loud and sudden knock
of the hotel dick—an art student
in her underwear, her dungarees with the
rolled up cuffs half lying on a chair
an arrogant poet of twenty-five naked
and hiding in the closet hardly breathing
the suitcase with the bricks inside and only
meant to delude the gatekeepers
the vice squad ready to do its duty,
the management ready to throw us out,
Duke Ellington somewhere, somewhere a car
standing in an alley, words everywhere,
words on the windshield, words in the snow,
but we shivered in silence on the bed
then we spoke in French
for it was a dear thing.

Limping

Space again for a predatory wasp
to sing you to sleep and good cracks in the sidewalk
where the trees spread year by year creating broken
steps either up or down and two garages
from 1929, I know it as sure as
I know the hollow blocks though I'd have to
get into urban archeology from
Pittsburgh east as well as the decades and that's
not my job, though I don't know what my job is,
mourning, finding a word, finding
a number—8—showing what's despicable,
clearing the air, remembering, though not official,
I'm not official, I just ingest,
devour, I said once "reconciling
two oblivious worlds," I said "getting ready,"
naming names, maybe it's
hiding behind a tree, maybe
getting inside the tree, maybe
learning to love the one or two breeds of dogs
I didn't love before—say boxers, say stiff-haired
small brown crossbreeds, say it's
walking again as far as the Flea, say it's
limping, even if I don't have to.

Oaxaca

Call it the bus they used to carry workers
and thieves alike both going to work or God
knows what or ten hands reaching down to pull you
up so you could hang on to the slats
and feel your upper teeth going into your brain
as first you slowed going up to give the gears
a chance to find the grooves then shaking
as they dropped into third though there was a strong
smell of sweat—and urine—in it, given how
you were crowded together, your leather suitcase
taking up too much room, the next hill
shaped like a parrot, the color
the color of bamboo, that perfect orange going
into yellow and leaving red, another bus
just behind you, shaking and groaning, finding
every hole, the thieves and workers it seems
jumping together, no one falling, though who was
bleeding or screaming I can't remember, it being
the year a Wilson was one of the Secretaries
and he had a hat made out of paper money
fifty dollars with President Grant on one side
looking as if he were walking in his sleep
in Riverside Park, near his tomb, I saw him
several times, I know it's hard to believe,
two thousand miles north of the flowering hills.

THE TRUTH

He was carried out of himself since he
had bells and he was given to screaming
and when the time came he reached over his head
to pull the cord, and he walked mostly sideways
for he had been a crab once and the cakes he
walked on were sometimes covered in snow and sometimes
mud, and everything floated then and sometimes
he held the cakes—I'll call them islands—together
with his shoes or the muscles above his knees
and that was a dance that made him forget
he was a crab, the truth was he wore
taps, and his pants were short, and he could fly
from cake to cake, for he had wings, and a feather—
I'd call it longing, maybe I'll call it frenzy.

LOVE

A wet towel so many times you'd think
I'd finally get it, say the day
I reached into my pocket for two hundred fifty
with nothing in writing and forty more for the paint
though it was more for Jack Daniel's and Jim Beam;

or say the day I made the mortgage payment
to save a house and made an agreement for working
against the money, involving receipts and deadlines,
but both were ignored, and who paid the next month's mortgage
there's no way of knowing;

                        but money is only water,
isn't it, and everything rises and falls and
somehow it's only smoke but the poorer poor
reach down on the sidewalk for a penny, bohemians
too, they know exactly what's in their pockets
down to the dollar, for they are provident,
unlike the bastards who don't need pockets since
the tailors cut their pants without to give a
smooth ferocious look like the Czarist police,
or the corporate piggery eating and vomiting;

and one time I picked up a soul near Easton, P.A.,
and drove him down to my house and cooked
an omelette you can't imagine—with Big Boy tomatoes
out of our garden and new potatoes and drove him
downstream to catch a bus to Philadelphia
and probably gave him twenty bucks besides—
the day of hopeless amour on the Delaware.

CONFLATING THE LIVES

Harry Stern

By whose obedience I was directed in my own living
and introduced to the world of literature that way,
and broke my small dog's heart by feigning death
and put toilet paper on my own face to stop the bleeding;
and knew Studs Terkel whom I loved and Lionel Trilling
whom I didn't but neither Herbert Marcuse nor Mary McCarthy;

and made up for my own ignorance by criminal journeys
and lived with my three older sisters by sitting at the foot of the table
and taking only the smallest cuts to demonstrate submission

and continued through two long lives to become undivided,
which formerly I could only do through rage,
such being the time it takes in America to become a true Cossack.

MANURE SPREADER

It took an hour to start the machine but when it
trembled in our hands we knew the shit would
fix his roof and keep his marriage going
and loved—we loved—taking turns or each one
holding a handle and running down the furrows
keeping the monster erect but I loved most
bending forward shouting shit and chaining
some bastard in back and making him run
faster and faster, his mouth open, his glasses
turning brown, for I was godless then
and godless it was that helped me through this life
though you should see the godly, I don't know where
to start for that for they have huge buildings
but most of all they have choirs, and hold their
hands just so, one day I'll lie down and tell you.

Top of a Mountain

You could mistake the wind itself for a voice
though no one ever said it was a tenor
or not or even male or female although
without even blinking you knew, and it was mostly
unequivocal though I wanted the words,
even if it was the wind, for which, well,
a pine tree took me in her arms the way they
do and we did Fred Allen and Arthur Godfrey
and other voices back of the bus and such,
the pine tree too before we both got serious
and put our hats on, me with a Lindy, both ears
covered in flaps, she with a rag, a kind of
bandage, and referenced Job and Jeremiah
and I said "Perish the day" but didn't mean it
for I was lucky, I said so once, and I did
swaying, the pine tree too, though maybe
she swayed first, stunted as she was,
but don't worry, I won't be struck dead
for my poetry, I'm too old for that,
and if I'm too loud it's all about the things
I'm trying to find the word for—murder, greed—
a single word, contamination, scandal,
moaning—though that's personal—even swaying, even
if I'm surrounded by others, even if I
caress the suffering branches, for I have permission.

HELL

Jones & Laughlin

It was easy to call it that because of the
smoke pouring through the bricks or just the
bricks themselves burning and we kept picking up red-hot
chunks and where we could we reinforced
the outer walls above and below our heads,
and who and what we were we couldn't exactly
tell for we were covered in soot and hopped
away from the heat like hot dancers
for we were creating flames for those on the mountain
who drove up the steep sides to see the view
and took their visitors with them so they could express
their gratitude, though no one up there knew
that we wore thick white Tom Mix gloves with the word
"diamond" imprinted on the cuff and a large
red star as if on the knuckles and we were juggling
the burning bricks and our hands were blistered
and after a while our thick black shoes were steaming,
talk about inner and outer circles, talk about
Virgil whose name was something from Eastern
Europe near the Carpathians, soup out of cabbage,
meat out of fat, garlic from dog-star roses.

BUFFALO

Wear a buffalo's head
let fleas drink from your eyes
and let the horns go blazing
through that eccentric debris
for the traces that crisscross
the continent, let it come
from nowhere oh and give him
long lashes above the black eyes
so the dust doesn't worry and sting him
though what buffalo in his right mind
could lift his hoof and remove
a speck from his own eye
with or without a handkerchief
save one whose tongue alone
was eaten by a white man
who left the rest to rot
we learned in Elementary.

MEDICINAL

I gave thanks of a sort that there were waves,
green oil or not, and that the bridge was low
and made of wood and that the ride was longer
than I expected; and I had time afterward
to put it together again, whatever the name of the
swamp was, though I drove myself crazy
trying to figure out what the dirt road was
and if the flower I picked was medicinal,
and was it the tiny round head or the long root,
and could I save a life? Not to mention
the mystery of the small cement building
and where the driver himself came from—
was he the one from Thessalonica,
a Turk as I recall, and was he the one
who wore a necktie with green on one side
and brown on the other that bore a screaming eagle
with bolts of lightning coming from the claws
your grandfather wore in the early thirties
when he did curbside at Idlewild.

MULE

What good did it do him to sit in the white tub
and soap his back with a curved brush? He was
a mule who circled around the monstrous stone
from right to left, dragging and grinding and wearing
the blinders, and one time he tossed the hay
over his head and turned his teeth to one side
to catch it the way a mule does, bending to eat
the sweet and tasty grasses, and that's when a stick
of sorts was used to guide him; you should have seen him
weighing tomatoes, in spite of the welts,
you should have seen him unloading bituminous coal
with a long shovel, pushing it down the chute
the way he and his kind did every winter
for twenty-five cents a load, give or take some.

What Happened to G.S.

Here is the Hole and here is the Sledge Hammer
you have your choice
since I am your guardian.

We don't practice beating the genitals here
with metal pipes or removal of teeth with pliers
or dislocation of fingers; also you can
eat and drink what the others do
but you have to sit alone with me.

My favorite song is "Now the Day Is Over,"
  "Shadows of the evening
  steal across the sky."

Only I am no longer your guardian
now that I have a knife in my chest.

PART II

WILDERNESS

Given how deer are pests now
you'd think it was no big thing watching one
run up Union Street at six in the morning
in the middle of town looking for a woods
though he may have smelled the river, which only confused him—
at least that's what I think—and he turned right
on Jefferson toward the hills, if you consider
the corner where an impatient woman was running
in place and we went softly in different directions
for we were too ashamed to look at each other.

TRACT

I was about to throw a chair at my mother
when I decided it was much better
to spill gravy on her tablecloth
but the only way I knew how to do it
was to dismantle everything,
which is why I pulled the cloth from under the chicken,
and for this reason I will walk to my own grave weeping
at the back of my coffin as WCW advises.

Not Me

It wasn't me but someone else in his eighties
sitting against a wall and it had to be
his mother sitting beside him well over a hundred
and maybe blind—I couldn't tell—and feeding her
from a tin plate or maybe it was foil
of some kind—I don't remember and when
a small girl maybe three or four came by
in tan stockings with horizontal blue stripes
and new blue shoes—and sunglasses I remember—
it could have been Crete—Heraklion, I'm sure of it
he stared in disbelief, maybe in envy,
maybe even in joy, and turned to his mother
to whisper something and folded his stiff fingers
over his belly and broke out into a smile
and half closed his eyes and almost nodded,
there were so many decades between them—
he could have slapped the ground with gratitude.

CARDBOARD

Consider cardboard for a while,
how you fitted it into your shoe
laboring over it with a scissors,
and making adjustments, say the long toe,
say the first curve on the left—
or just neglect—and how you could stick two fingers
altogether through the sole, you almost
could start there and rip the shoe apart,
which was something else from the four sores you suffered
when the shoes were new and from the vertical
climb where only steps would work and you
leaned half over to see the cars parked
at the foot of the hill, and looking up there was
from time to time a single cloud, which you
could have taken for something else if you weren't so tired.

After Ritsos

One man stood apart and announced to the others
it was a form of hysteria and explained
to them the roots and connections to a woman's body.

But it was only when they brought the donkey over
to comfort her that she stopped her screaming
and gradually turned to sobbing in response to
which a dozen handkerchiefs appeared,
and everyone explained things to his neighbor
but the donkey loved her more than the man did,
he who was looking for a tree to rub against.

And there was an unearthly sound he made
as he backed up against a wooden post
to ease the sores on his haunches,
and I was remembering my own donkeys
and the kindness of Anne Marie.

AFTER THE CHURCH READING AGAINST THE WAR

It was Galway kept talking about the sidewalk
and how it was made of stone and not cement
and what a great wonder it was to him,
but there was old snow piled up and I had to
walk in the street against the cars mostly
speeding cabs and I would have stood my ground
if someone there didn't pull me away although
what I remember I jumped over a barrier—
I sort of flew—and my pride knew no
bounds but at the restaurant I was too quiet
and maybe they thought I hurt my back or I was
thinking of death but I had probably
zeroed in on nothing, which no one can stand;

and it was such a pleasure driving home
with the window open and the smell of
winter on Route 78 and thinking
again of Galway and his stone sidewalk
and how I flew and how a bird ascends
at the last minute just to tease you, especially
crows, especially pigeons—and sparrows—so hungry
they stay for the bread and only when you reach down
do they go for the blue, and though it wasn't blue that night
but black, with snowflakes falling on your eyelids,
and though you did the bread later you flew
first over a red plastic fence, then over a wooden
and if there was only a starter wind to lift you
you might have never stopped flying, you might have *risen*.

BEING THIRTY

for Asta

Usually I delivered yellow pages from
June to September for Donnelly but one year
one of the senior professors blew his brains out
in the presence of his terrified wife
and that freed up his course that summer so we could
move brazenly into eating meat;

and by the way I bought a sofa that summer
for thirty dollars on Pine Street in Philadelphia
and lashed it to the roof of my Volvo and all the
way home—in the rain—the plastic kept blowing
over the windshield and I leaned hard to the left
in my idiocy to balance the weight and
twice I stopped to retie it the first time a parking lot
in Ogontz I think, the second time in New Hope,
gray mohair where once Myrna Loy stretched out
tipping ashes from an ivory cigarette holder
and William Powell leaned down to pick the dog up.

In the Kitchen

I want to say I am the one who knows
but what good is knowledge in whatever form it takes
for it can't exist by itself like a brain in alcohol.

Two things come to mind, don't they, the
size of the brain and the size of the famous member,
Einstein and Byron.

Then there was Abie the ape from one of my earlier years
and if I say this you will wince with horror
but he was after the daughter and he needed
someone to keep the mother company.

I thought I could hear him laughing in the bedroom
like a wild ass at home in the wilderness
as Jeremiah said,

and, in the kitchen, where I held the mother,
I had the knowledge but I wept for her.

112TH STREET (1980)

Where there used to be a telephone booth here
that's where she stood banging on the glass
wearing only a raincoat over her slip
accusing him of calling another woman
when he was only halfway out the door
and he was embarrassed when he recovered from
the shock and he tried to protect her from the shame
and couldn't believe her rage and how her eyes
flashed as if in a drugstore novel and he
embraced her while she covered her face with her hands
and he remembered it thirty years later with something
like shame himself—though they both laughed later—
but something was lost, especially when he walked
by the building where the phone booth used to be,
and she would suffer bouts of sickness and death,
quick and unexpected and obdurate—
what they never dreamed about—fighting
each other two hundred feet over the river.

LINOLEUM

Those were elephant prints
and not red linoleum,
thank God for that, I never
could stand linoleum, give me
most of all a pine floor,
pitch pine from southern
New Jersey is fine, and if
there is a ragged rug
as thin as could be even
threads showing, what does it
matter? And maybe a jar
with a lid that fits just right
and a signature near the bottom,
something from central Iowa
I have dragged here and there—
and anything from the forties,
including sinks and canisters
or the heavy typewriter
I carried from country to country
the gray metallic surface I
loved so much, the ribbon
drooping like a loose stocking
but I won't get into
the old design of lamp shades,
I'll just say a double
helix, as in the ear,
and let it go at that
for what's the difference as long as
there's no linoleum;
I used to squat on a hole

in the days of *Henri Quatre*,
the nights of Sylvia
from Budapest, a river
flowing through her, I was
swimming south, she had castles
for thighs, there was a chain bridge
she used as a belt, she wanted
to come to America, she was a
Jew lost in Paris, she
wanted to marry me but
I was already in love with
Ilana Shmueli from Czernowitz,
a name that sounds amusing,
a city that sounds amusing
to our Anglo-Saxon ears
that hate Slavic syllables,
especially endings, she left
on the last tub from Romania—
the other two sank—and stayed
in an English concentration
camp in Palestine
and lived in Israel for sixty
more years but never learned
Hebrew properly—she studied
Greek while wearing the star
and taught herself Yiddish
since Jews from Czernowitz
only spoke German
as if they were in Vienna
living with lace doilies
and learned the violin
playing every day though practically
starving, she was instructed
by Paul Celan who lectured on

Villon, Baudelaire, Rimbaud,
eighteen years old already
while she was fifteen and living—
like him—in a Nazi ghetto,
and they took dangerous walks
in the public gardens
outside the ghetto;
and met him again in Paris
twenty, thirty, years later
and slept with him and listened
to his poems and tried to nurse him
and read her own to him
I spoke to by telephone
maybe a year ago
in Tel Aviv and we were
making plans for her to
come to New Jersey but then
she died and we never talked
linoleum nor double
helixes and she hated
Bibi the dangerous pedantic
fool who played football—
you won't believe it—
in high school outside
Philadelphia they called
Benny the bully, smoke that,
fact checkers for the *New Republic*—
I would have met her plane
and rented a Lincoln for her,
I would have given her water
then let her sleep awhile
on the way to the hotel
in Madison, New Jersey,
her first room in America.

WIND AND WATER

There was a way of living under a pier
to study sand and water for even then
there was a certain choppiness as well as a
long give-and-take and in the puddle
there was a dirty rainbow but the sun,
which burned my feet a minute before could hardly
get through the cracks and it was cold and dark
underneath the planks and there without
knowing it, and mostly at noon
when I unwrapped the wax and ate my sandwich,
I heard footsteps over my head as one board
rumbled from the loose nails
and I had the pleasure of living in two places
and one was a kind of cave, sand and water
shifting with the time of day, and sometimes
there was such cunning and clarity under the
pier it could have been a garden.

Free Lunch

I don't give a damn who gets a free lunch
in the first Methodist church on Union Street,
I just wish they'd fix their roof and let us
alone for a while, though you can tell a *schnorrer*
because he looks around and then puts
two quarters in the jar instead of say
a sawbuck and looks so happy leaving
as if he'd just put one over on the canary
or the wild volunteer in the orange apron, but your
heart would go out to the large-headed woman
who picked up her doll from a wooden high chair
and carried it out September 11, 2012.

And for God's sake, someone bring up Isaiah
who had his faults amen but
refused to budge and he was sawn in half
at the end and someone bring up Debs
who ran for president five times
on the Socialist ticket and the last time
got a million write-in votes while serving
time because he hated war and said that
while there's a lower class, he was in it,
and while there's a soul in prison, he was not free,
and so on, so where's his stamp, post office?

SEXUAL

It was easy enough for a tree to groan in such a wind
and leaves to scold and even to fall
and for a while the air was suddenly warm
as if the sky would burst and what had been
a growing darkness would reverse itself
as the least sun broke in over the edges.

It was, I'd say, sexual if you could use that word
to describe an act of nature, to do it that way,
terrifying in its way
and isolated, that's the word that comes to me,
everyone in it only for himself,
like someone in his twenties, only
you're in your eighties now and you shouldn't be doing this.

I'm going to go to this place twice a week
for I love the Methodists since they used to believe
in *plein air* just like the first Hasids
in Lithuania, Poland, and Russia,
although it turns out September 12th was the day
I ate my meatballs not September 11th,
and I am fighting full disclosure with all my might
for a poem is like a woman in her 50s.

NANCY

What extravagance
going crazy over little things
me with my black locust
barely a branch I harvested
from the weeds growing near my water,
you with your mower
cutting everything down
running over the small circle of stones
I surrounded the tree with
for you had poor eyesight
or you couldn't hear me
or you were just singing.

And what's it called pouring water over my own head
and rubbing myself with oil?
And what were the useless trips you made to my house
sometimes twice a week, called Maintenance?
And what were the false negotiations we had,
under my redbud,
the first called "utter frustration,"
the second "mystification?"
And what did it mean bringing me an eggplant one day
and peaches the next?
And where has the unbearable fragrance gone
in the center of my garden
and when will you be ready to get on your fours
and eat straw like an ox?

Schissel[1]

It was as if my feet were being washed
and there was a man with a red skullcap
on his knees in front of me or maybe
leaning over and breathing hard, his face,
what I saw of it, red; and white hair
for fringes, which makes me hold the two beasts
together and curl my toes for I never asked
for soap and hot water and though I rolled my pants
up to the knees I closed my eyes so as not
to see his delicate fingers and likewise separate
honor from dishonor, and if he had looked up
just once I would have bent half down to kiss him.

---

1. Yiddish word for "bowl" or "basin"

Joan's House

Loving the mirrors on the ceiling at Joan's house,
loving her rebirth trying to do it
sideways both of us lying on our backs
both of us blind the light fixture just like a breast
the sixties gone the seventies halfway over
one of her sons in prison, one son cutting
himself, David I think it was, my own son
still in high school days of the Afro her roommate
putting up a mirror herself her boyfriend
helping her, brilliant sullen Kevin he was
a witness he and Evelyn they held hands we
hated the Colonels most her island I know was
directly south of Sparta Sinatra was president.

MARYANNE

Everyone gets her day, Maryanne whom I
talked to exactly thirteen months ago
it seems was more at peace than anyone else
and though she had twenty-three cats and lived in rural
Arkansas I remember her curled up
as we say and reading old Cambodian novels
on the sixth floor—I think it was—while Howard
raged here and there and I am grateful we got
back in touch after 55 years and I am
amazed they lived together again, he with his
castle in Burgundy and his young French wife,
she with her puffed up eyes and her black dresses
though both of their phones are dead now.

Havanese

Nobody tells me I owe them a kiss
or for that matter what kind of kiss I owe them,
whether wet or cheeky or on the eye
holding the head between my two hands
and should the eye be closed or not
and where I came from I made the rules
and it was I who wore my shoulder out
carrying bag after bag and in my time it was paper,
not that hopeless plastic made from shitty
oil squeezed out of shale, and *I* had the children
and *I* carted them and by the way it was *I*
who held the dog in my lap
the Havanese with the flat Maltese nose
who herded chickens, I hear, the way Border collies
do sheep—and cows—and people—nipping, barking,
for which you should be standing up and holding your mouth open
for there are nine kinds of kisses
and three are sexual.

FUSION

He was hungry for the Automat,
the bookstores on Fourth
and the pile of wrinkled shirts at Klein's.

It was a voice that followed him
and made him hold on to a brick wall.

But he wouldn't settle for anything like vertigo,
he of the grand reflexes,
who felt humiliated by his huge feet.

All of it came to a head
the night the Marshall Plan was explained
disgracefully by Gabriel Heatter

     "There's good news tonight
      Yes, there's good news tonight."

Or Walter Winchell

     "Good evening, Mr. and Mrs. North America
     and all the ships at sea,
     Let's go to press!"

Oh, strange fusion.

BREAKING FREE

Put your nose to the grindstone, love
you are tied to an old perfection,
trapped in a cafeteria.

Here we go again with an abandoned telephone pole
trying to break down a door.

Watch your step, just think of it as a rope
and get to your place in front
and spit on your hands for luck
and breathe through your chest, as Miss Steiner insisted.

What Brings Me Here?

Here I am again and what brings me here
to the same wooden bench
preaching to the city of Lambertville
surrounded by mayapples?

For who in the hell is going to lie down with whom in the hell,
either inside or outside? And you know it's amazing
to watch flies lie down with feces
or mosquitoes lie down with blue bloods
and over there is a double house you call a twin
and when the one on the right burned down in under a minute
the one on the left refused to budge, not even an inch.

I'm not saying a French horn with a trombone
or a fleabane with a fleabane

or in one case
wood as fuel with wood as a god.

And I'm not saying it doesn't matter,
grinding the faces of the poor,
or whether it's a song or not.

Even if someone got carried away
and swam across the East River to Little Poland;

even if someone called himself a remnant
and lay there for sale cheap in the cheapo bin

whose grandfather had a trumpet for an ear
and raged against the heartless
then lost his polished head lying down with the sycamores.

IDA

I could never see her as someone who plucked
feathers or who labored out of a bowl
or, like her mother, stick her hand inside a bird's
cavity to remove the yellow eggs, but
someone who sat in a window seat to read
Tolstoy or meet her father who came
to get her after work and walk her home
so there should be a man beside her;
and she was a queen of train stations
and long good-byes she picked up from her reading
and I learned regret from her and
had the "blues," but I
spent a half day walking instead of biting
the end of a Turkish towel or a rolled up washrag;
and now I'm waiting to see which one will outlive
the other and what the next five years will bring
though Tolstoy died in a train station
caught between preaching and acting and thus
choking to death from what they called pneumonia,
but I can say that though I admire his thinking—
and his last journey—my own journey
will be a lot less philosophical and a lot more
sensual and I will avoid train stations—maybe
I will move to Key Largo for I loved
the fish sandwiches there and the swimming pools.

DURANTE

How could I ever lie down like that
listening to Jimmy Durante singing "Try a Little Tenderness"?
Wasn't there a war on and weren't legs being sawn off
by second lieutenants right out of medical schools
in Pittsburgh and Philadelphia, home of Montefiore (in one case)
and Albert Einstein North and Albert Einstein South (in the other)?
and wasn't my back getting tired carrying so much in
and out including celery and Raisin Bran and 8 O'Clock
and once a sofa and twice an upright piano and
wallboard out of my open trunk my body bent
forward a little and my elbows taking the weight, my
neck itself the telltale repository
of a hundred different pains, each one
enough to slow a gorilla down; and I should
love the mattress itself, which I have been sleeping on
for thirty-three years and I should have fixed the record player
and I shouldn't have put the box of records on the curb
and lose the voices that way, and I should have paid
a sixteen-year-old to lift my end of the piano
and I shouldn't have been so arrogant carrying
all alone a 4 by 8 3/4-inch wallboard
and I should have played patty-cake with the gorilla
and I should have let Louise carry her own sofa
or I could have carried the two cushions
and put them back in place on the open porch
waiting for the truck to park in the flower bed.

"I'll Be Around"

flip side of "Paper Doll"

We were talking about it for ten minutes
when I decided just to sing it for that's
what it was for as buildings are for living in
and stoves to cook on and books to read
and it's a big deal and children under five are right
when they hold a curved wooden spoon up
to the light and ask what it's for, though I do like
Alec Wilder breaking the record over his knee
because the Mills Brothers had changed the chord progression
and, like him—like everybody—I scribble words
on the back of envelopes and for that reason
and for two others which I'm too considerate to mention
I'll be around when you're gone.

The Memory of a Meal

Who cares now if he chose to live
the other side of the river or whether
he reconstructed fish bones
just for the memory of a meal
or whether a thick soup
out of gizzards and neck bones
or—like Henry Miller—he had a system of
free-loading and whether Miller
was grateful to Lowenfels
for supper once a week or if he critiqued
the chicken as too tough or too lemony—
so exquisite his taste—the great
sexpot who knew nothing about women
and called it the Noble Prize in one of his home
movies, sitting on the throne of honor;
and where my mind took me
or maybe just my pencil for I lean on
the carbon, but it's only in pity
of Lowenfels who lived in the Pine Barrens
when he came back from France and one night his cabin
was surrounded by ridiculous FBI agents
with their guns drawn
from which his wife Lillian suffered a stroke
and he was taken away in chains although
he didn't even have a BB gun, or even a
sharpened knife, not even a stick, and he was
a lyric poet who shared an early prize with
E. E. Cummings, though when he was three
he joined the Party for he was ashamed
of his father's money and after all he read

Amos—didn't he—something about the Smith Act
and overthrowing the U.S. Government
or just thinking about it, that was enough,
or maybe they didn't like his mimosa bush
we visited in Weymouth, New Jersey,
Jack Lindeman and I, the selfsame cabin
by the Mullica River the summer of
1957 we brought down herring and
pumpernickel bread he sliced a tomato
from his garden and made us coffee
heavy with sugar and cream and he wore puttees
in WWI and just like Lindeman
trapped in Belgium he was in infantry.

If you could only have heard Louise singing
from Cole Porter and Johnny Mercer and holding
her hands just so, the way Miss Steiner taught us
while she was waiting for the horn to catch up
and resting her fingers on the brushed velvet
as if it were Jane Eyre; though it would be a
big deal even to leave Pittsburgh
and catch the bus for New York City where she could
dance up the escalator and through the newspapers
with Fred Astaire, she was so much in love
with the thirties and forties though her main secret
was "September Song" and her main love was
Kurt Weill though mine was
"Skylark," it made me catch myself so,
ghost that I was, I who had nothing
to mourn for yet, neither words nor music.

Roebling

Living on this river and being close to
the Roebling Bridge, with the Riegelsville Hotel
on one side and crazy Hoots on the other,
it's like you're being protected or even embraced
by someone carrying a huge tomato in his hands
walking on the meshes by the rails;
and you can lecture at will to poor Jeremy
on John Roebling and the Brooklyn Bridge
and how a suspension bridge was constructed
and what his wife and son and daughter-in-law did
after he died to further the construction
and how I used to cross this bridge going back
and forth on my way to work, four, five, times a week,
and when the train came south, and how it hauled paper
from Riegel and how my friends and I collected
discarded sheets and rolls of paper and how I still have
some of the sheets and so on, for we were walking
on the meshes too and looking down at the
water though it could have been someone else
carrying a tomato, for every god has a river.

THE WORLD WE SHOULD HAVE STAYED IN

The clothes, the food, the nickel-coated iron
flower tables, the glass-and-wood-fluted doorknob
but most of all the baby girls holding
chicks in one arm and grapes in the other
just before the murder of the Gypsies
under Tiso the priest, Slovak, Roman-Catholic,
no cousin to Andy, he Carpatho-Russian
or most of all Peter Oresick, he of Ford City,
he of Highland Park and East Liberty
Carpatho-Russian too, or just Ruthenian,
me staring at a coconut tree, I swear it,
listening late on a Saturday afternoon
a few weeks before my 88th to
airplane after airplane and reading the trailers
by the underwater lights of yon organ-shaped
squid-squirming blue and land-lost swimming pool
the noise a kind of roar when they got close
I'm watching from the fifth floor up, Warholean
here and there oh mostly on the elevator but
certainly by the pool, his European relatives
basking under his long serrated leaves
coconuts near the top—ripe and dangerous—
like Peter, coming from one of the villages inside
Pittsburgh, like me, half eastern Poland, half southern
Ukraine, born in the Hill, on Wylie Avenue,
the first village east of downtown Pittsburgh,
Logan Street, the steepest street in the Hill,
two blocks—at least—a string of small stores and
Jewish restaurants, Caplan's, Weinstein's, I was
born at the end of an era, I hung on with

my fingers then with my nails, Judith Vollmer's
family was Polish but they were twelve miles away from
Peter's village, this was a meal at Weinstein's:
chopped liver first or herring or eggs and onions, then
matzo-ball soup or noodle or knaidel, followed by
roast veal or boiled beef and horseradish
or roast chicken and vegetables, coleslaw
and Jewish pickles on the side and plates
of cookies and poppy-seed cakes and strudel,
Yiddish the lingua franca, tea in a glass,
the world we should have stayed in, for in America
you burn in one place, then you burn in another.

He spent nine years living among the apples
complaining daily that his shower was on the first floor,
shaving, as he recalled, on the second,
eating breakfast in sight of the redbud.

In the third year he picked one up to smell it
and was transported at once to upstate New York
or his uncle George's farm in Mars, P.A.,
inhaling in both places with his eyes closed.

After he sold the house to his plumber he came back
to see what she had done with the backyard
and to understand how a little rottenness had done him in
though actually he drove down the deeply rutted alley
and forced his way past the mulberry tree
through the crowded white lilacs just to eat one;

after which he would bend down for a nickel
though theretofore he said a dime—or a quarter—
and this is the way he learned to enrich himself
coming to New York on a cheap train
and sitting all night in thought, worms included.

PART III

DIVINE NOTHINGNESS

I have to say I can't find the *Book of Brightness*
anywhere, not Amazon, not even the library at
Princeton, though I almost scream at the librarian
"it was carried across the border
from Provence into Spain and Portugal
and tied with hemp under the warm saddle
of the wisest donkey east and north of Madrid,"
and for herself I show her my ten fingers
and explain the separations and what the messages were
and how the years of baseball had interfered
through breakage and swelling now permanent and how
there are ten candles waiting to be lit
and what the permutations and distortions were
and how I wasn't crazy but had to find
the book to round out my education
and I was losing faith in Princeton, what with the
shoes and dresses in the windows and I could have
gotten in touch with the unfathomable
if only Princeton had it and I gave her the
title in Hebrew as well as a short lecture
and what came out of what but I had to go through
the glass doors with nothing but an egg sandwich
wrapped in plastic the way it used to be wrapped
in wax paper and either go down to Trenton
or figure out the permutations by myself
and I blamed Allen Ginsberg for all this
since I know they had the *Book of Pure Suffering*
written in the same century as *The Brightness*.

I insist that Miriam was the mother
and not the sister for we do the great lies
in order to make a narrative flow or
not to be embarrassed by the secrets
of bastardy and this would partly explain
the discovery of the abandoned baby
in the royal basket, and for all you know,
she and Aaron and Moses could represent
ah, different beliefs or nations, particularly Aaron,
and the nomenclature "brother" could be a *metaphor*,
and I don't think Freud got it either, not here.
Wasn't the central fact that Him on High
wouldn't disgrace Himself by showing His back side
to a woman, especially one who worshipped a cow?

OLD WAR

In the war on opossums it was Cicero
the hater of pouches, who led the charge, not
because they were so ancient but since they
were hopeless breeders and bore their young
two weeks after conception and not only that
but ate what was rotten and had long noses and beards
and played with death, as we all know; and it would be
easy to kill them, say in Germania, since
they would inhale the gasses quietly but
what did Cicero know of that, he who
called them noisy, ill-mannered, exclusive,
inhuman and blamed them for mob action
and the control of gold just as in later years
they would be blamed for their bad Latin
and flowery neckties, so weird and unfitting
it all was; and if you go to Williamsburg
you will see exhausted females with their babies
clinging to their backs, their manicured fingers
opening the refrigerators and turning on the stoves
for they have thirteen sources, it is written
in the books, it goes back three thousand years.

MOUSE TRAP

I had to call my daughter to get the name of
the ball of fur my former wife and I
delivered to the animal rescue, the countryside
outside of Easton, hills nearby, and trees;
for she remembers the names of all our cats
and had a small graveyard outside my study
above the river, and the ball of fur was Mouse Trap
she who deposited rats and moles at the kitchen
door for her contribution; and some of the others
were Peter Rabbit who broke his leg falling
out of a tree, and Pickles who ran away
and Cookie and Ollie and Herbie we put away for
renal failure and Willie my daughter said was pure white
and hit in the snow by a car and Calico Cousin
who also was hit, her face was ruined and she hid
in a closet—the way cats do—I was the only one
who fed and petted her and finally Nimbus the
watch cat, who walked visitors to
our front door and he was killed one Labor Day
I buried before my family got up, in the woods
down the road; but Mouse Trap jumped out of my arms
as if a sixth sense told her what was happening and
disappeared in the woods and fields I called the
countryside and I am sure she was the
scourge of all the small things, including birds
I'm sure, and we returned two times to look for her—
I had a '66 Volvo—but it was useless for
she had blended already and I suspect
her claws were busy though I *half* suspected her
to show up one day for cats are good at that

but after a week I gave up looking, this was
forty years ago but murder was then the
same as now, whatever the names of the cats were,
however childish—wherever the graveyard was—and Julia
who's only eight this year already knows that.

MONGOLIAN

I have to say I am *not* a Mongolian
in spite of my upper body strength and my folded
eyelids but rather my family traveled north
from Spain to Provence—mostly by night since it was
dangerous and the route was lit by a book
quietly burning for the whole two days though
nothing was consumed and this was called
the Gift of the Book we celebrated the
anniversary of the day we entered the
southern reaches of France, and we picked up
French first then German on the Rhine
and came to Poland during the Third Crusade,
und so weiter, this book I have kept hidden—
with some other valuables—it is for
the Great Emergency, which should not come
in the next two hundred years and as for the question
"what's inside the book?" I have lost the first
of the five languages now I am relearning.

FALLING

He was given to falling, he who walked
on air shaking a blue oilcloth or
slipped on silk down pine and maple steps
or leaning on a wobbly kitchen chair
and staring up at the light and what his specialty was
was letting his bones take over, what he called
relaxing, even on his coccyx, and blue and
black were his colors, with a tinge of red,
blue more than black, red more than blue,
at least in his one-way mirror, and one time he was
"cleaning" and one time he had lost his shoes,
and never on ice and never on a mountain,
he who grew up on a cliff, he who walked—
ran—from a Swiss lake to Venice and walked
thence to Bologna, he who climbed all day
in the city his grandfather came to, likewise it had
tunnels and even bridges—likewise rivers,
but mostly dirty fish and small crocodiles.

Maybe you should marry a Spirit, maybe you should
be impolite, maybe you should guard the
entrances—that's what Shelley meant—
guard the entrances—Blake said it too—
don't let pigs in, that's what we said,
don't pollute the sidewalks, don't throw newspapers
into the bushes, you could occupy anything
you wanted, and as far as acknowledgment
here's a prize for your adverbs and here's one
for your prepositional phrases, name a prize
after your favorite Spirit, applaud yourself and
introduce yourself or just introduce
the first introducer, then you get your prize
somewhere down the line, you have to decide
whether *unacknowledged* is the thing or if
it's *legislator*: which can you abide?
You could say "abide with me,
fast grows the evening tide,"
or you could let the will take over as Nietzsche
advised, or you could just
let the Spirit do it, after all you
married her, she made the coffee, she sliced
your chocolate croissant, she *engaged* you,
she knows one thing from another she won't
let you be a fool, she is your guard dog, your ghost.

THREE SHARP SOUNDS

What does a titmouse want with me
since heretofore it has been only
cardinals and blue jays, with an occasional murderous
robin, but I am going by *sound* this early,
my yard, the woods beyond, the
river, though I am in a small city more
in the country, more by water since you have to count
the canal as well where wood and coal from upstate
Pennsylvania floated down on barges—into the '20s
I read—and wasn't there a titmouse on the prow
and wasn't it so tame that one of the children,
say near Stockton, put two fingers out for
a limb of sorts—and didn't it peck at the limb
and make its three sharp sounds?—I have read that too.

MARK'S PHOTO OF K.B.

Kenneth Burke is holding his right hand up
to his forehead—he's thinking—or suffering—
his ears are large, his hair is white and his striped
brown shirt is so much like my own I am
astounded, his mouth is open and his eyes
are closed, he is writing four books at once,
he finally has an indoor toilet, he
thinks every day of Malcolm Cowley, he loved
Hart Crane, he hated Eliot, Roethke told him
he was a lousy poet, he said fuck you
to Foucault, he met him at a talk
at Oberlin, Mark Hillringhouse told me this.

One of her feet was on top of her own head
the other pushed against the thigh for leverage
though I couldn't figure out which leg was what

nor have I ever seen legs that long
or a body so double-jointed and contorted
nor can I even tell you what she's lying on

though the blanket itself is a deep red
and the background is a dark blue,
whoever Michael Allan Wilkinson was

and what she was to him
and how he could put her legs in the air like that
and how he got her to do it,

three years before I was born.

1944

I don't remember her name now but that's normal
just as it was "normal" during a black-out drill for the lights
to be extinguished and the blinds to be pushed against the
windows just in case, as it was likewise for his mother
to scream out his name over the sirens—for him to
return home since how could it be safe next door
with only the flat-chested large-eyed girl there, *her* mother
out somewhere and the two of *them* on the sofa together
both breathing between kisses and him about to board her—
no other word could do considering how thin she was and how
burly he was—and the term for it was dry-fucking
though his mother kept up her screaming until he gave up
and walked—was it twenty steps?—back to his own
house, for how could he bear his own name in the tree-
tops and the wires—just hanging there—like a torn
kite, the strings tangled and the strips of cloth that
fought the wind stuck somewhere and the second syllable
of his name like an accusation: unforgiving, deadly, lost,
just outside the two small houses. I would
say like a blue jay's wing if I didn't already say a kite.

TRANSPORT

I'm the polar opposite of my old friend and
fellow Pittsburgher (according to J.M.) the latter
"circumspect with wonder," while the former,
(that would be me) "supercharged with it," though how
you could be "supercharged" with wonder as if a device
were forcing air into your carburetor I don't know,
but I suppose a Ford or even a
Chevy could be full of ebullience, joy and energy,
without temperance or austerity, and I'm in a state of
rapture and, of course, *transport*—even a Packard,
the second one down from the top in the days of
ecstasy, when I was a windy lad and a bit.

Three Stages in My Hometown

You'd think it was a weird idea for a dirty river
and at least they'd have to put some medicine in it
although it was the *words*, it was what they said
and not the water itself, just as they lit the street lamps
as early as 2 p.m. to let the light in
on their foul work, just as we gave in
on certain days in August and held our breath
although we should have covered our faces for there was
a smell and sometimes something sharp and greasy,
even slippery, given the sky, though it was
different the next day, starting at midnight and after
the next next at the Italian club and the
Serbian, for both had accordions and twelve feet
of polished wood or on the *following* morning
our facial hair gone and tight flowery neckties
or stockings and dresses, inside the stone Gothics
listening to the so-called words of the dead Jew.

DEATH 2013

I know what, I'll grieve for the redbud
that didn't blossom this year,
for the dead limbs and the handful of leaves
that on the left side, while looking down
shook ever so slightly in the vicious wind;
or better yet, I'll grieve for the bark I
tore off in handfuls, loose and unsupported
or for the drowned ants in my sink
or the tiny white animals with black babies
under them that, in the thousands, infested my hemlock,
I mean the tree itself, infested thus, or just the
wood at the bottom of the verticals
that were—whilom—a fence. Is Sylvia
still encased in her rotten satin shroud?
Are those babies hers?

BLUE SANTIAGO

I have called it by so many names
I am finally disgusted with the whole thing

you had to be a registered nihilist
or wear a wide-brimmed black hat

while waiting for the Polish King in Brooklyn
or the lifeguard at Lakewood sitting on his royal ladder

or some kind of marriage, half dog, half fox,
and if a fox the one who lived underneath

the wooden porch and didn't budge no matter
how close you got, her twelve or so pounds

half covered in dust
her fur matted and mangy

from eluding the bloods
her teeth—except the rippers—half-rotten

from crushing rabbits,
her eyes bloodshot, her body exhausted

her last stand there, at Little Bighorn, at Stalingrad,
but the dog don't matter.

Much Better Than a Goat

Much better than a goat it was to drop
an anarchist from a Park Row window
because he wouldn't confess to federal agents.
He fell to his death while sitting on the windowsill
holding a pamphlet close to his eyes and maybe
waving his arm in appreciation, and no one
heard him screaming—they were wearing earmuffs
or just they forgot to bring their earpieces
but it was nothing, he was a fiend and a cutthroat
and he would have murdered Rockefeller if he had the chance,
for which reason I have locked my front door
for I can't find a rat trap big enough.

He Who Is Filthy

He who has a forehead
will have a forehead still,
and she who has a little brown egg
will have her nest and give her milk
in the most unlikely place of all;
and Johnny Cash will sit with his hand
on one leg and his other hand holding his head up,

and Learned Cohen will get on his knees
before his brilliant violinist;
and he who is filthy will be filthy still
and most of all, Thelonius Monk
will turn around again and again,
a different tic from mine
but equally respectable.

OUT OF THE BLUE

I know I'll go down in history without a hotel
but how I would have loved to come home in the evening
and collect my mail from the slots in front
and go up the elevator to a clean and vacuumed room
say the size of the ones at the Hotel Earle
two rooms for the price then of only seven dollars
including a bath including a living room including
a table between the windows and no Bible in the drawer
turned into a welfare hotel in the '70s turned into
the Washington Square with rooms the size of a bathroom
a country mile away from the place of loneliness
grief and joy, a coffee shop on the ground floor
and services galore. I'll have to tell you
one day how I brought a woman in there
and the clerk was astonished and how a pipe was leaking
and how she wept but that was another matter
1972 I'd say she called me out of the blue Sunday morning.

Good to lie down in a yard of shadowing bimbo trees
against a dying redbud near a Japanese maple
whose deliquescent branches year by year
it gets darker and darker.

Good to be near a fence which unlike its neighbors
both up and down it's all of wire a see through
chain-link different from the wooden walls,
the jails nearby, the swimming pools and sling chairs.

Good to be here finally filling in the gaps
and drinking coconut milk again
and out of debt forever.